BREAKING FREE

An Anthology of Human Rights Poetry

Selected By Robert Hull

Wayland

First published by Wayland (Publishers) Ltd
61 Western Road, Hove, East Sussex BN3 1JD,
England

© Copyright 1994 Wayland (Publishers) Ltd

Editor: Katie Roden
Designers: Susie Hooper and Joyce Chester
Cover designed by Malcolm Walker

British Library Cataloguing in Publication Data
Freedom: Anthology of Poetry
I. Hull, Robert
808.81358

ISBN 0-7502-1031-1

Typeset by Dorchester Typesetting Group Ltd,
England
Printed and bound in Italy by G. Canale and
C.S.p.A., Turin

Acknowledgements
The publishers would like to thank the
following for allowing their pictures to be used
in this book:
Camera Press 14, 41 (Sven Simon), 45 (Benoit
Gysembergh), 47, 55 (Dick Saunders); Robert
Harding/FPG International 26; Impact Photos
7 (Philip Littleton/Reflex), 10 (Dod Miller), 13
(Caroline Penn), 18 (Steve Benbow), 28 (Peter
Ashell), 29 (Benny Gool), 49 (Jane Greening),
53 (Peter Ashell), 57 (Caroline Penn); Imperial
War Museum 42, 56; Link Picture Library 17
(Greg English); Tony Stone Worldwide 15;
Topham Picture Source 8–9, 11 (Mark
Antman), 21, 31, 32, 59; United Press
International 46; UNRWA *title page* (Emile
Andria), 22, 39 (George Nehmeh), 52 (Myrtle
Winter Chaumeny); Wayland Picture Library
19, 24, 34, 37, 40, 48, 50; Zefa Picture
Library 27.

For permission to reprint copyright material the
publishers gratefully acknowledge the following:
Anvil Poetry Press Ltd for 'The Need For Censorship',
by Reiner Kunze, translated by Michael Hamburger
from *The Poetry Of Survival* edited by Daniel Weisbort,
published by Anvil Poetry Press Ltd; Constable
Publishers for 'Red Cockatoo' and 'The Little Cart'
from *170 Chinese Poems* by Arthur Waley. Reprinted by
permission of Constable Publishers; Faber and Faber
Limited Publishers for 'Refugee Blues' from *Collected
Poems* by W H Auden. Reprinted by permission of the
publishers; Forest Books for 'The Village' by Ana
Blandiana from *Anthology of Contemporary Romanian
Poetry* translated by Andrea Deletant and Brenda
Walker. Reprinted by permission of the publisher;
Claire Grierson for 'Freedom Is...'. Reproduced by
permission of the author; David Higham Associates for
'Ballad of the Landlord' from *Selected Poems of Langston
Hughes* by Langston Hughes. Published by Vintage;
'The Hand That Signed The Paper' by Dylan Thomas
from *Poems of Dylan Thomas*. Reprinted by permission
of David Higham Associates for the UK and New
Directions Publishing Corp. for the US Copyright ©
1939 New Directions Publishing Corp.; Alfred A.
Knopf Inc. for 'Negro' from *Selected Poems* by Langston
Hughes. Copyright © 1926 by Alfred A. Knopf Inc.,
renewed 1954 by Langston Hughes. Reprinted by
permission of the publisher; The National Exhibition of
Children's Art for 'Boxes' by Joanne Yates and
'Discipline' by Claire Milne; Oxford University Press for
'I Watched an Eagle Soar' by Virginia Driving Hawk
Sneve. Copyright © 1989 Virginia Driving Hawk
Sneve. Reprinted from *Dancing Tepees: Poems of the
North American Indian Youth* edited by Virginia Driving
Hawk Sneve (1989). Reproduced by permission of
Oxford University Press; Penguin Books Ltd for 'Wings'
from *Selected Poems* by Miroslav Holub, translated by
Ian Milner and George Theiner. Translation copyright
© Penguin Books Ltd, 1967; Random House UK Ltd
and Princeton University Press for 'Walls' by C P
Cavafy from *Collected Prose* translated by Edmund Keely
and Philip Sherrard, published by The Hogarth Press;
Random House Inc. for 'Refugee Blues' from the book
Collected Poems by W H Auden Copyright © 1940 and
renewed 1968 by W H Auden. Reprinted by permission
of Random House Inc.; 'Mama Dot' from *Mama Dot*
by Fred D'Aguiar, published by Chatto & Windus;
Reed Book Services for 'The Democratic Judge' trans-
lated by Michael Hamburger and 'The Burning Of The
Books' translated by John Willett from *Poems
1913–1956* by Bertolt Brecht. Reprinted by permission
of Reed Book Services; Three Continents Press for
'Twenty Comrades' and 'I Shall Sing' from *The Wind-
Driven Reed* by Fouzi El-Asmar. Reprinted by permis-
sion of the publisher; The University of Michigan Press
for 'Here is Klito's Little Shack' by Leonidas, translated
by Kenneth Rexroth from *The Greek Anthology*,
reprinted by permission of the publisher. While every
effort has been made to secure permission, in some cases
it has proved impossible to trace the copyright holders.
The publishers apologise for this apparent negligence.

**The Glamorgan Centre for
Art & Design Technology**

Contents

INTRODUCTION

Two students were dining in a restaurant. One raised his glass: 'To freedom!' The other also raised his glass. 'To freedom!' For that, they were arrested and sent to prison for seven years. It happened not in a story, not in some ancient cruel empire, not even in Nazi Germany or Russia in the 1930s, but less than forty years ago in Portugal, a country some of us might go to for holidays.

In tyrannies, life runs on fear. Fear of strangers, neighbours, colleagues at work, friends. Fear of the secret police, secret prisons, secret executions; of arrests, searches, disappearances. A Chilean poet wrote, 'Nobody could walk through the avenues without terror bursting through their bones.'

For us, who are free from such horror, it's hard to imagine how normal fear-ruled worlds can become. But no harder, perhaps, than for people in freer countries not to notice the freedoms that surround them getting thinner, draining away.

Words can mislead us into thinking everything's normal. 'The free world', 'a free country', we say, as if freedom were one thing or one quality. Just as we still say 'free as air', forgetting that even the air is less free than it was – less free from carbons, sulphur, CFCs, and the rest. The air of freedom can become polluted without our noticing. When politicians lie to us, that fouls the air. We become, without knowing it, less free.

The poet Blake had a phrase for it – 'mind-forg'd manacles'. Freedom starts to die in the head when people allow others to chain up their brains. A Greek politician had the same thought: 'A tyrant enslaves a people through their ignorance.' And it's easy to be ignorant. Just stop thinking, reading, bothering, arguing. Don't ask awkward questions. Don't rock the boat.

Words themselves can manacle the mind. I discovered a horrific expression while researching for this book – 'humane torture'. Whoever invented that phrase was turning words upside down. So was whoever called a prison in Uruguay 'La Libertad'. The inhuman is human, prison is liberty, so up is down and hate is love and these words are not words.

The reason why tyrants chain the mind with upside-down words is fear of the truth. Many of the poems here either were, or still are, banned in the countries where they were written. Because they unchained the mind; they told the truth.

The body has chains too. The Chilean poet Neruda writes of the 'poor, poor man' who had 'neither house, nor land, nor alphabet, nor sheets, nor meat to eat'. The poor man might have been free to say what he liked and go where he liked, but not free from hunger, poverty or homelessness. And these things are made more terrible by war. In many countries what people long for most is to be free from the terror of death and destruction.

Perhaps there are two kinds of freedom, freedom-from and freedom-to. Freedom from war, famine, injustice, tyranny; and freedom to do the things we think life is for – freedom to love, learn, work, create, travel. We need our freedoms-to, but it's hard to have them unless first we're secure in our freedoms-from.

In this selection of poems we see the tyrants' attempts to destroy the passion for freedom. In the end they don't work: 'You can exile it to Siberia and it will cry out with the voice of Ivan Denisovich'. The end is too late for those whom the torturers mutilate and kill, and for the families of the 'disappeared'. But poems get written; the longing for freedom never disappears. The Russian poet Osip Mandelstam died in a prison camp in Siberia, but he knew his poems would live after him:

> You took away all the oceans and all the room.
> You gave me my shoe-size in earth with bars around it.
> Where did it get you? Nowhere.
> You left me my lips, and they shape words, even in silence.

Translated by Clarence Brown
and W S Merwin

A worker in Durban,
South Africa.

THE BIG ROCK CANDY MOUNTAINS

On a summer day in the month of May,
A burly little bum come a-hikin',
He was travelin' down that lonesome road,
A-lookin' for his likin'.
He was headed for a land that's far away,
Beside those crystal fountains,
'I'll see you all, this comin' fall
In the Big Rock Candy Mountains.'

In the Big Rock Candy Mountains
You never change your socks,
And the little streams of alkyhol
Come a-tricklin' down the rocks.
Where the shacks all have to tip their hats,
And the railroad bulls are blind,
There's a lake of stew, and whiskey, too,
And you can paddle all around 'em in your big canoe,
In the Big Rock Candy Mountains.
   O . . . the . . . buzzin' of the bees
   In the cigarette trees,
   Round the sodawater fountains,
   Near the lemonade springs,
   Where the whangdoodle sings
   In the Big Rock Candy Mountains.

In the Big Rock Candy Mountains,
There's a land that's fair and bright,
Where the handouts grow on bushes,
And you sleep out every night.
Where the box cars are all empty
And the sun shines every day,
O I'm bound to go, where there ain't no snow,
Where the rain don't fall and the wind don't blow,
In the Big Rock Candy Mountains. (*Chorus*)

In the Big Rock Candy Mountains,
The jails are made of tin,
And you can bust right out again
As soon as they put you in.

The farmers' trees are full of fruit,
The barns are full of hay,
I'm goin' to stay where you sleep all day,
Where they boiled in oil the inventor of toil,
In the Big Rock Candy Mountains. (*Chorus*)

Traditional American folk song

Heading for Los Angeles,
USA, in 1937.

FREEDOM IS . . .

Like a leaf blowing freely,
   Like a bike doing a wheelie.
Like a fish swimming a stream,
   Like a gymnast on a beam.
Like a hawk soaring through the air,
   Like a big wheel at the fair.
Like a cat chasing its tail,
   Like the wind, rain and hail.
Like a kite up in the sky,
   Like a bee zooming by.
Like a flower soaking up the sun,
   Like a toddler having fun.

Claire Grierson (England)
(aged 13)

BOXES

My brother would put me in a
   SHUT-UP-JOANNE BOX
because I speak a lot.

My mum would put me in a
   TURN-ON-*NEIGHBOURS* BOX
because she likes it.

My dad would put me in a
   GO-TO-BED BOX
because he wants me to get out of his way.

My teacher would put me in
   THE WORK BOX
because I never do my work.

My friend would put me in
   THE SAME BOX AS HER
because she likes me.

     Joanne Yates (England)
        (aged 8)

DISCIPLINE

One times one is three.
Six times seven is forty two.
Battle of Hastings: 1066.
    Answer!
Grey dawn outside.

Who was the first disciple?
Define a primary source.
Hydrogen, helium, lithium . . .
    Answer!
Cloudy morning outside.

A quadrilateral is a four-sided shape.
An adjectival phrase describes a noun.
Eight quavers in a four-four bar.
    Answer!
Rain slithers outside.

Je suis, tu es, il est . . .
Repetition intensifies descriptive passages.
Denote recessive genes: *b.*
    Answer!
Stormy afternoon outside.

One of the themes of the play is gemstones.
Use the subjunctive with *il faut.*
Dress carefully for interviews.
    Answer!
Shadowed twilight outside.

Have you done last week's accounts?
Where is the Brown file?
Don't forget to clock in.
    Answer!
Weekend. Paycheque.
Darkness falls outside.

Claire Milne (England)
(aged 15)

WALLS

With no consideration, no pity, no shame,
they've built walls around me, thick and high.
And now I sit here feeling hopeless.
I can't think of anything else: this fate gnaws my mind –
because I had so much to do outside.
When they were building the walls, how could I not have noticed!
But I never heard the builders, not a sound.
Imperceptibly they've closed me off from the outside world.

C P Cavafy (Greece)

*Guards patrol the walls of
London's top security prison,
Wormwood Scrubs.*

I WATCHED AN EAGLE SOAR

Grandmother,
I watched an eagle soar
high in the sky
until a cloud covered him up.
Grandmother,
I still saw the eagle
behind my eyes.

Virginia Driving Hawk Sneve (USA)

THE RED COCKATOO

Sent as a present from Annam –
A red cockatoo.
Coloured like the peach-tree blossom,
Speaking with the speech of men.
And they did to it what is always done
To the learned and eloquent.
They took a cage with stout bars
And shut it up inside.

Po Chü-I (China)

A ROBIN RED BREAST IN A CAGE

A Robin Red breast in a Cage
Puts all Heaven in a Rage.

William Blake (England)

*Separate toilets for
black and white men
in Johannesburg,
South Africa, in 1983.*

KEEP OFF THE GRASS

The grass is a green mat
trimmed with gladioli
red like flames in a furnace.
The park bench, hallowed,
holds the loiterer listening
to the chant of the fountain
showering holy water on a congregation
of pigeons.

KEEP OFF THE GRASS,
DOGS NOT UNDER LEASH FORBIDDEN.

Then madam walks her Pekinese,
bathed and powdered and perfumed.
He sniffs at the face of the 'Keep Off' sign
with a nose as cold as frozen fish
and salutes it with a hind paw
leaving it weeping in anger and shame.

Oswald Mbuyiseni Mtshali (South Africa)

I NEVER HEAR THE WORD 'ESCAPE'

I never hear the word 'escape'
Without a quicker blood,
A sudden expectation,
A flying attitude!

I never hear of prisons broad
By soldiers battered down,
But I tug childish at my bars
Only to fail again!

Emily Dickinson (USA)

WINGS

There is
the
microscopic
anatomy
of
the whale
this is
reassuring
– William Carlos Williams

We have
a map of the universe
for microbes,
we have
a map of a microbe
for the universe.

We have
a Grand Master of chess
made of electronic circuits.

But above all
we have
the ability
to sort peas,
to cup water in our hands,
to seek
the right screw
under the sofa
for hours

This
gives us
wings.

Miroslav Holub (Czechoslovakia)
Translated by George Theiner

EQUAL OPPORTUNITY

in early canada
when railways were highways

each stop brought new opportunities

there was a rule

the chinese could only ride
the last two cars
of the trains

that is

until a train derailed
killing all those
in front

(the chinese erected an altar and thanked buddha)

a new rule was made

the chinese must ride
the front two cars
of the trains

that is

until another accident
claimed everyone
in the back

(the chinese erected an altar and thanked buddha)

after much debate
common sense prevailed

the chinese are now allowed
to sit anywhere
on any train

Jim Wong-Chu (Canada)

South African women protesting against apartheid in 1952.
They have locked themselves into a first-class carriage that
would usually be reserved for white people only.

THE DEMOCRATIC JUDGE

In Los Angeles, before the judge who examines people
Trying to become citizens of the United States
Came an Italian restaurant keeper. After grave preparations
Hindered, though, by his ignorance of the new language
In the test he replied to the question:
What is the 8th Amendment? falteringly:
1492. Since the law demands that applicants know the language

A Palestinian refugee registers his details in East Jordan. He fled here after his home was destroyed.

22

He was refused. Returning
After three months spent on further studies
Yet hindered still by ignorance of the new language
He was confronted this time with the question: Who was
The victorious general in the Civil War? His answer was:
1492. (Given amiably, in a loud voice.) Sent away again
And returning a third time, he answered
A third question: For how long a term are our Presidents elected?
Once more with: 1492. Now
The judge, who liked the man, realized that he could not
Learn the new language, asked him
How he earned his living and was told: by hard work. And so
At his fourth appearance the judge gave him the question:
When
Was America discovered? And on the strength of his correctly
   answering
1492, he was granted his citizenship.

Bertolt Brecht (Germany)
Translated by Michael Hamburger

COLONIZER'S LOGIC

These natives are unintelligent –
We can't understand their language.

Chinweizu (Nigeria)

COLUMBUS

*'Generally it was my wish to
pass no island without taking
possession of it.'*

The slaves were not profitable
'for almost half of them died'

but there were spears to be had
for broken crockery

and untouched rings of islets
like trinkets.

And though the Great Khan
finally went missing

and the gold pagodas
faded with the mists

there was the first flamingo
pink as dawn

there was the terminal innocence
of rivers.

When enough naked harbours
had been manacled

enough grief
requisitioned

a cargo of fables
set out for Spain, heavy

with lilting names –
Cathay   Indies

conquistadores   spices
syphilis.

Robert Hull (England)

*The Spanish explorers treated
the native South Americans
like slaves after landing in the
'New World' in 1492.*

IF ONE WANTS THAT BIRD

You know,
there was a king in Mongolia,
      who once invaded some
distant kingdom, where
he heard a new bird singing,
and wanted the song for himself.
For the sake of the song, he wished to capture
the bird, with the bird its nest,
the branches that held the nest,
the trunk of the tree, the tree itself,
the roots, the earth that held the roots,
the village,
the water,
the surrounding land,
the country,
the entire kingdom . . .
      Wanting to take them all
he gathered together all the remaining
elephants, horses, chariots
and soldiers,
conquered the entire kingdom,
annexed it to his empire

and never returned home.

A K Ramanujan (India)
Translated by S K Desai

MAMA DOT

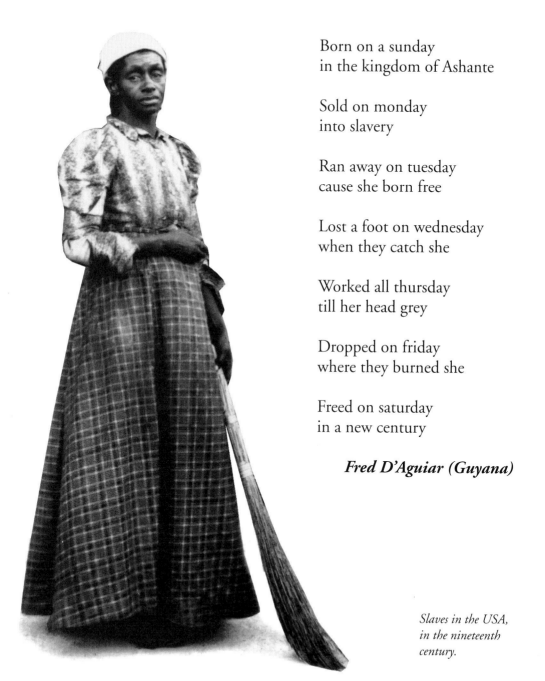

Born on a sunday
in the kingdom of Ashante

Sold on monday
into slavery

Ran away on tuesday
cause she born free

Lost a foot on wednesday
when they catch she

Worked all thursday
till her head grey

Dropped on friday
where they burned she

Freed on saturday
in a new century

Fred D'Aguiar (Guyana)

*Slaves in the USA,
in the nineteenth
century.*

NEGRO

I am a Negro:
　　Black as the night is black,
　　Black like the depths of my Africa.

I've been a slave:
　　Caesar told me to keep his door-steps clean.
　　I brushed the boots of Washington.

I've been a worker:
　　Under my hand the pyramids arose.
　　I made mortar for the Woolworth Building.

I've been a singer:
　　All the way from Africa to Georgia
　　I carried my sorrow songs.
　　I made ragtime.

I've been a victim:
　　The Belgians cut off my hands in the Congo.
　　They lynch me still in Mississippi.

I am a Negro:
　　Black as the night is black,
　　Black like the depths of my Africa.

Langston Hughes (USA)

RECEPTION

Going to prison
I can remember the discomfort
of being handcuffed. Doing my best
to keep up, we walked through the entrance
of the building they called Reception. To me
it looked more like the Accident Unit of some
hospital. 'Over here,' I heard a voice say.
Starting with my name
I emptied my memory onto the desk, each
detail meticulously noted. They began to
remove my belongings from me, one by one taking
away the things that made me different
from the next man. Each removal became for me
a reminder of the withdrawal
of my freedom.
Shirt, trousers, tie, socks, underpants, shoes,
taken and sealed in plastic, stripped
until I stood naked before them. They gave me
prison blues and said 'Put these on.' A doctor
asked 'Are you suicidal?' casually adding 'Do you
have Aids?' I said no, desperately wishing
someone would ask me
how I felt.

Colin Bartlett (England)

IN MY COUNTRY

In my country they jail you
for what they think you think.
My uncle once said to me:
they'll implant a microchip
in our minds
to flash our thoughts and dreams
on to a screen at John Vorster Square.
I was scared:
by day I guard my tongue
by night my dreams.

Pitika Ntuli (Azania)

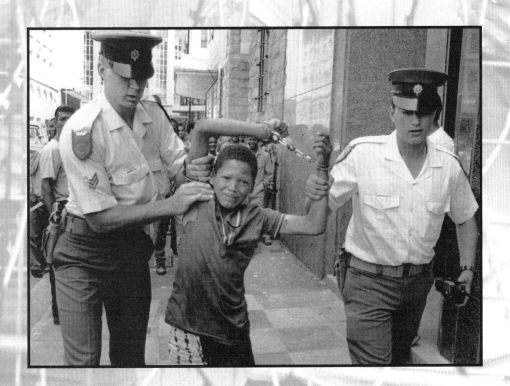

THE CENSOR

The Censor is seated on a stool (or possibly two stools).
The Dancer enters.
At a sign from the Censor she begins to dance.
Censor: More slowly, please.
The Dancer continues to dance.
The Censor stops her.
Censor: Hold it! Show me that last movement again.
The Dancer does so.
The Censor shakes his head.
Censor: No, no, no. Leave that out.
The Dancer resumes her dance.
Censor: No. Not that. Omit it.
The Dancer dances.
Censor: That's not allowed.
The Dancer again resumes dancing.
Censor: Omit!
(after a while)
   Omit!
(after a while)
   Leave out!
(after a while)
   And that!
The Dancer no longer dances, she is merely walking about the stage.
Censor: What's this? Call that a dance? Why aren't you dancing?
The Dancer shrugs her shoulders helplessly.
Censor: Don't do that!
The Curtain starts to come down.
Censor: Just a moment!
The Curtain stops.

Members of the Hitler Youth, the junior branch of the Nazi Party, burning books thought to contain anti-Nazi writings, in Salzburg, Austria in 1938.

Censor: I won't stand for any innuendo. Gently, now
 . . . that's better . . . gently . . . very, very slowly . . .

The End

Ivan Kraus (Czechoslovakia)
Translated by George Theiner

THE BURNING OF THE BOOKS

When the Regime commanded that books with
   harmful knowledge
Should be publicly burned and on all sides
Oxen were forced to drag cartloads of books
To the bonfires, a banished
Writer, one of the best, scanning the list of the
Burned, was shocked to find that his
Books had been passed over. He rushed to his desk
On wings of wrath, and wrote a letter to those in
   power
Burn me! he wrote with flying pen, burn me! Haven't
   my books
Always reported the truth? And here you are
Treating me like a liar! I command you:
Burn me!

Bertolt Brecht (Germany)
Translated by John Willett

THE NEED FOR CENSORSHIP

Everything
can be retouched

except
the negative
inside us

Reiner Kunze (Germany)
Translated by Michael Hamburger

SEARCH

Come in, Gentlemen – he said. No inconvenience. Look through everything;
I have nothing to hide. Here's the bedroom, here the study,
here the dining-room. Here? – the attic for old things; –
everything wears out, Gentlemen; it's full; everything wears out, wears out,
so quickly too, Gentlemen; this? – a thimble; – mother's;
this? mother's oil-lamp, mother's umbrella – she loved me enormously; –
but this forged identity card? this jewellery, somebody else's? the dirty towel?
this theatre ticket? the shirt with holes? blood stains?
and this photograph? his, yes, wearing a woman's hat covered with flowers,
inscribed to a stranger – his handwriting –
who planted these in here? who planted these in here? who planted these in here?

Yannis Ritsos (Greece)
Translated by Nikos Stangos

Police arrest a
demonstrator
against military
rule in Santiago,
Chile, in 1984.

HOPE

My son has been   missing
since May the 8th   of last year.
    They took him   just for a few hours
    they said
    just for some routine   questioning.
After the car left,
the car with no license plate,
we couldn't   find out
anything else
about him.

*Detained supporters of the Allende
government in Chile, after the
government was overthrown in 1973.*

But now things have changed.
We heard from a young compañero   who just got out
that five months later
they were torturing him   in Villa Grimaldi,
at the end of September
they were questioning him
in the red house   that belonged to the Grimaldis.
    They say they recognised
    his voice   his screams   they say.

Somebody tell me frankly   what times are these
what kind of world   what country?
What I am asking is   how can it be
that a father's   joy
a mother's   joy
is knowing
that they
that they are still
torturing
their son?
Which means   that he was alive
five months later
and our greatest   hope
will be to find out   next year
that they're still torturing him
eight months later

and he may   might   could
still be alive.

Ariel Dorfman (Chile)
Translated by Edie Grossman

HIS EYE IS ON THE SPARROW

Forgive us, Lord, for sending   this petition
but we have no place else to turn.
The Junta won't answer,
El Mercurio makes jokes and is silent,
the Court of Appeals will not hear   the defense appeal,
the Supreme Court has ordered us to   cease and desist,
and no police station
dares   receive
this petition   from his family.

    Lord, you who are everywhere,
    have you been   in
    Villa Grimaldi, too?

They say nobody ever leaves   the Colonia Dignidad,
or the cellar on Londres Street,
or the top floor of   the Military Academy.
    Have you?

If you have,
if you really are everywhere,
please answer us.
When you were there
did you see our son
Gerardo? Lord, he was baptised
in your church
Gerardo, the most rebellious, the sweetest
of the four.
If you don't remember him
we can send a snapshot
the kind you take in the park   on Sunday

and the last time we saw him,   right after supper,
that night when they knocked   on the door,
he was wearing a blue jacket   and faded jeans.
He must still be wearing them now.

Lord, you who see everything,
have you
seen him?

Ariel Dorfman (Chile)
Translated by Edie Grossman

Relatives pleading for the return of their
family members who have 'disappeared',
or been taken prisoner, in Chile.

TWENTY COMRADES

Beloved, you ask me
Of life in this prison, this cell
   what of the chains
chafing my wrists
   what of my food and drink
and the comrades of my cell?

Beloved, let me tell you:
Our clouds are indeed heavy
But our being here
is a smile of spring,
the shock of thunder
in autumn, after drought.
We are not defeated
as our jailers are.

Fouzi El-Asmar (Palestinian, now living in USA)

I SHALL SING

I shall create
out of the darkness of my jail
my dawn
out of the jaws of hatred
my destiny.
I shall sing
the wind
the sun
the flowers
the spring.
I shall sing
in spite of fences
in spite of jailers
in spite of hatred.

**Fouzi El-Asmar
(Palestinian, now
living in USA)**

*A Palestinian
refugee in Marka
camp, East Jordan.*

PAWIAK 1943

It was exactly eleven
steps from wall to wall
in the Pawiak Prison
from to from to
wall wall wall wall
and eleven and back again

I walked this

till today
for so many cramped years
if I set out
then I begin
with the twelfth step

Jerzy Ficowski (Poland)
Translated by Frank J Corliss Jr
and Grazyna Sandel

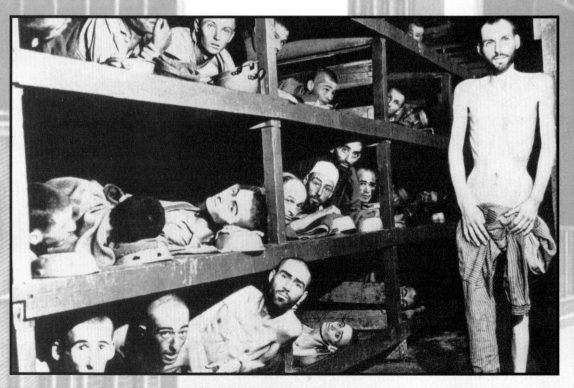

Prisoners in a Nazi concentration
camp in Poland during the Second
World War.

FROM: LA LIBERTAD

YOU should see
the contradictions there are
in the army
you should have heard
the arguments between
the sub-lieutenant and the captain
while they were torturing me.

Mario Benedetti (Uruguay)
Translated by Alicia and Nick Caistor

THE MOST UNBELIEVABLE PART

The most unbelievable part,
they were people like us
good manners
well-educated and refined.
Versed in abstract sciences,
always took a box for the Symphony
made regular trips to the dentist
attended very nice prep schools
some played golf . . .

Adolf Hitler, leader
of the Nazi Party.

Yes, people like you, like me
family men
grandfathers
uncles and godfathers.

But they went crazy
delighted in burning
children and books
played at decorating cemeteries
bought furniture made of broken bones
dined on tender ears and testicles.

Thought they were invincible
meticulous in their duties
and spoke of torture
in the language of surgeons and butchers.

They assassinated the young of my country
and of yours.
now nobody could believe in Alice through the looking glass
now nobody could stroll along the avenues
without terror bursting through their bones

And the most unbelievable part
they were people
like you
like me
yes, nice people
just like us.

Marjorie Agosin (Chile)
Translated by Cola Franzen

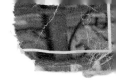

THE REASON

The reason why
murderers and thieves
so easily
become statues
are made into monuments
is
already their eyes are granite
their hearts
are made
of stone.

Chris Van Wyk (South Africa)

STRONG MEN DESTROY A CITY

Strong men destroy a city, and a tyrant
   enslaves a people through their ignorance.

Solon (Greece)
Translated by Willis Barnstone

SOMOZA UNVEILS THE STATUE OF SOMOZA IN SOMOZA STADIUM

It's not that I think the people erected this statue
because I know better than you that I ordered it myself.
Nor do I pretend to pass into posterity with it
because I know the people will topple it over someday.
Not that I wanted to erect to myself in life
the monument you never would erect to me in death:
I erected this statue because I knew you would hate it.

Ernesto Cardenal (Nicaragua)
Translated by Steven F White

President Anastasio Somoza of Nicaragua.

SONNET: ENGLAND IN 1819

An old, mad, blind, despised, and dying king,—
Princes, the dregs of their dull race, who flow
Through public scorn,—mud from a muddy spring,—
Rulers who neither see, nor feel, nor know,
But leech-like to their fainting country cling,
Till they drop, blind in blood, without a blow,—
A people starved and stabbed in the untilled field,—
An army, which liberticide and prey
Makes as a two-edged sword to all who wield,—
Golden and sanguine laws which tempt and slay;
Religion Christless, Godless—a book sealed;
A Senate,—Time's worst statute unrepealed,—
Are graves, from which a glorious Phantom may
Burst, to illumine our tempestuous day.

Percy Shelley (England)

*A demonstration by the unemployed during
the Great Depression, in England, 1931.*

THE STALIN EPIGRAM

Our lives no longer feel ground under them.
At ten paces you can't hear our words.

But whenever there's a snatch of talk
it turns to the Kremlin mountaineer,

the ten thick worms his fingers,
his words like measures of weight,

the huge laughing cockroaches on his top lip,
the glitter of his boot-rims.

Ringed with a scum of chicken-necked bosses
he toys with the tributes of half-men.

One whistles, another meouws, a third snivels.
He pokes out his finger and he alone goes boom.

He forges decrees in a line like horseshoes,
One for the groin, one the forehead, temple, eye.

He rolls the executions on his tongue like berries.
He wishes he could hug them like big friends from home.

Osip Mandelstam (USSR)
Translated by Clarence Brown

A statue of Joseph Stalin.

THE HAND THAT SIGNED THE PAPER

The hand that signed the paper felled a city;
Five sovereign fingers taxed the breath,
Doubled the globe of dead and halved a country;
These five kings did a king to death.

The mighty hand leads to a sloping shoulder,
The finger joints are cramped with chalk;
A goose's quill has put an end to murder
That put an end to talk.

The hand that signed the treaty bred a fever,
And famine grew, and locusts came;
Great is the hand that holds dominion over
Man by a scribbled name.

The five kings count the dead but do not soften
The crusted wounds nor pat the brow;
A hand rules pity as a hand rules heaven;
Hands have no tears to flow.

Dylan Thomas (Wales)

DESCRIPTION OF AN IDEA

You can nail it to a cross
and it will rise again after three days.
You can put it in the arena with several wild beasts
and it will survive its own dismemberment.
You can tie it to a stake and light faggots under it
and the crackling of the flames will speak volumes.
You can exile it to Siberia
and it will still cry out with the voice of Ivan Denisovich.
You can beat it to a bloody pulp in a public square in Peking
and it will still think of freedom.
You can turn the Star Chamber and the SS
    and the KGB and the Savak
        and the State Security Bureau
           loose on it
and someone somewhere will still think it
and someone somewhere will still die for it
and someone somewhere will give it new life.
For an idea is an organism more mysterious in its action
than the miracidium.
. . . You can declare an idea anathema to 999,999,999 people
and the billionth will reach for a dictionary . . .

Bruce Dawe (Australia)

*A student demonstration in T'ien-an
Men Square, Beijing, in 1989. Many
students were massacred by the army
during this demonstration.*

REFUGEE BLUES

Say this city has ten million souls,
Some are living in mansions, some are living in holes:
Yet there's no place for us, my dear, yet there's no place for us.

Once we had a country and we thought it fair,
Look in the atlas and you'll find it there:
We cannot go there now, my dear, we cannot go there now.

In the village churchyard there grows an old yew,
Every spring it blossoms anew:
Old passports can't do that, my dear, old passports can't do that.

The consul banged the table and said,
'If you've got no passport you're officially dead':
But we are still alive, my dear, but we are still alive.

Went to a committee; they offered me a chair;
Asked me politely to return next year:
But where shall we go to-day, my dear, but where shall we go to-day?

*Jewish people being taken
from their homes by Nazi
soldiers in Germany, during
the Second World War.*

Came to a public meeting; the speaker got up and said;
'If we let them in, they will steal our daily bread':
He was talking of you and me, my dear, he was talking of you
    and me.

Thought I heard the thunder rumbling in the sky;
It was Hitler over Europe, saying, 'They must die':
O we were in his mind, my dear, O we were in his mind.

Saw a poodle in a jacket fastened with a pin,
Saw a door opened and a cat let in:
But they weren't German Jews, my dear, but they weren't
    German Jews.

Went down the harbour and stood upon the quay,
Saw the fish swimming as if they were free:
Only ten feet away, my dear, only ten feet away.

Walked through a wood, saw the birds in the trees;
They had no politicians and sang at their ease:
They weren't the human race, my dear, they weren't the
    human race.

Dreamed I saw a building with a thousand floors,
A thousand windows and a thousand doors:
Not one of them was ours, my dear, not one of them was ours.

Stood on a great plain in the falling snow;
Ten thousand soldiers marched to and fro:
Looking for you and me, my dear, looking for you and me.

W H Auden (England)

THE LITTLE CART

The little cart jolting and banging through the yellow haze of dusk.
   The man pushing behind: the woman pulling in front.
They have left the city and do not know where to go.
'Green, green, those elm-tree leaves: *they* will cure my hunger,
If only we could find some quiet place and sup on them together.'

   The wind has flattened the yellow mother-wort:
   Above it in the distance they see the walls of a house.
'*There* surely must be people living who'll give you something to eat.'
They tap at the door, but no one comes: they look in, but the
     kitchen is empty.
They stand hesitating in the lonely road and their tears fall like rain.

Chēn Tzŭ-lung (China)
Translated by Arthur Waley

After the 1948 Arab-Israeli war, many refugees found shelter in tents and caves.

LONDON

I wander thro' each charter'd street,
Near where the charter'd Thames does flow,
And mark in every face I meet
Marks of weakness, marks of woe.

In every cry of every Man,
In every Infant's cry of fear,
In every voice, in every ban,
The mind-forg'd manacles I hear.

How the Chimney-sweeper's cry
Every black'ning Church appalls;
And the hapless Soldier's sigh
Runs in blood down Palace walls.

But most thro' midnight streets I hear
How the youthful Harlot's curse
Blasts the new born Infant's tear,
And blights with plagues the Marriage hearse.

William Blake (England)

BALLAD OF THE LANDLORD

Landlord, landlord,
My roof has sprung a leak.
Don't you 'member I told you about it
Way last week?

Landlord, landlord,
These steps is broken down.
When you come up yourself
It's a wonder you don't fall down.

Ten Bucks you say I owe you?
Ten Bucks you say is due?
Well, that's Ten Bucks more'n I'll pay you
Till you fix this house up new.

What? You gonna get eviction orders?
You gonna cut off my heat?
You gonna take my furniture and
Throw it in the street?

Um-huh! You talking high and mighty.
Talk on – till you get through.
You ain't gonna be able to say a word
If I land my fist on you.

Police! Police!
Come and get this man!
He's trying to ruin the government
And overturn the land!

Copper's whistle!

Patrol bell!
Arrest.

Precinct Station.
Iron cell.
Headlines in press:

MAN THREATENS LANDLORD

TENANT HELD NO BAIL

JUDGE GIVES NEGRO 90 DAYS IN COUNTY JAIL

Langston Hughes (USA)

Children in Harlem, New York, playing outside a run-down apartment block.

FROM: TO THE DEAD POOR MAN

We will bury our poor man today: our poor poor man.

He always went round so badly
it's the first time he's been housed.

Because he had neither house, nor land,
nor alphabet, nor sheets, nor meat to eat,
and he went around like that,
on the roads, from one place to another,
dying from having no life,
dying little by little,
because this had lasted him since birth.

Luckily, and it is strange,
everyone from the bishop to the judge agreed
in telling him he would go to heaven:
and now dead, well dead our poor poor man.
He won't know what to do with so much heaven.
Will he be able to plough it, and sow it, and harvest it?

He always did, he fought hard with the ground,
and now the sky is soft for ploughing,
and later among the heavenly fruit
he'll finally have some of his own.
Seventy years of hunger to be satisfied at last,
without him getting any more blows from life,
without him being locked up for eating.

This man never hoped for such fairness;
suddenly they have filled him up and he's grateful:
he already went silent with happiness.

How heavy our poor man is now!
He used to be skin and bone and black eyes,
and now we know, just from his weight,
how many things he went without; and
how much we never defended him on earth.

Pablo Neruda (Chile)
Translated by William Levin

HERE IS KLITO'S LITTLE SHACK

Here is Klito's little shack.
Here is his little cornpatch.
Here is his tiny vineyard.
Here is his little woodlot.
Here Klito spent eighty years.

Leonidas of Tarentum
(Greece)
Translated by Kenneth Rexroth

A VILLAGE

More of a smell
Than image or sound,
The smell of smoke in the evening,
Especially when the herds return, dizzy
From too much milk flowered in the fields;
Smell of milk making a froth,
Pulled erotically from the udder, as if
Coupling in its blue flesh
The green soul of wild grass
With the gentle, moving
Breath of smoke;
The smell of wet straw
And heaps of berries,
Smell of wheat pyramids rising to the sky,
While the air of evening seeps back into itself
And clouds unfold
Into brief stories and vanish;
The smell of self,
Of hair long in the sun,
Of skin for herbs dreaming,
Of sleep and of word –
A village built on air
From endless seeming,
Loved with one's breath
And rocked by the wind!

Ana Blandiana (Romania)
Translated by Andrea Deletant and Brenda Walker

PEACE

Peace is the odour of food in the evening,
when the halting of a car in the street is not fear,
when a knock on the door means a friend

Peace is a glass of warm milk
and a book in front of the child who awakens

Yannis Ritsos (Greece)
Translated by Nikos Stangos

NOTES

Walls (p.14) C P Cavafy (1863–1933) was one of the most important Greek poets. He strongly criticized traditional values such as Christianity and patriotism.

I Watched An Eagle Soar (p.15) Virginia Driving Hawk Sneve grew up on the Rosebud Sioux Reservation. She now lives in Rapid City, South Dakota, USA. She has written several novels about Native American characters.

The Red Cockatoo (p.16) Po Chü-i (772–846) was born into poverty and rose to become a high-ranking minister. His simple-seeming poems were so popular that he sometimes found them written on the walls of temples and lodging-houses where he stayed.

A Robin Red Breast in a Cage (p.16), ***London*** (p.53) William Blake (1757–1827) was a poet, painter and mystic.

Keep off the Grass (p.17) The poetry of Oswald Mbuyiseni Mtshali (1940–) describes his experiences of apartheid in South Africa. Apartheid is the keeping apart of black and white people by, for example, making them live in different areas, go to separate schools and use separate parts of the public transport system.

I Never Hear The Word 'Escape' (p.18) Emily Dickinson (1830–1886) is one of the most famous poets of the nineteenth century. Her poems, with their simple, hymn-like forms, are very powerful.

Wings (p.19) Miroslav Holub, one of the world's great poets, was born in 1923 in Czechoslovakia, where he was also a leading scientist. His poems are often about politics and the loss of freedom under tyranny. He wanted his readers to read poems 'as naturally as they read the newspapers', and some of his best poems can be read in just that way.

The Democratic Judge (p.22) Bertolt Brecht (1898–1956) was a German poet, playwright and pioneer of new forms of theatre. In his writing he criticized the upper classes and the military. During the Second World War he went into exile in Scandinavia and the United States. In Germany, his books were burned by the Nazi Party. The Eighth Amendment refers to a section of the US Constitution, the laws written in 1787. The Eighth Amendment says, 'Excessive bail shall not be required, nor excessive fines imposed, nor cruel and unusual punishment inflicted'.

Colonizer's Logic (p.23) This poem refers to the settlement of a country by another people, and their ignorant attitudes to the native inhabitants of that country. Chinweizu is a Nigerian poet and writer.

If One Wants That Bird (p.25) A K Ramanujan is a well-known translator, poet and collector of stories. He is a professor at the University of Chicago.

Negro (p.27), ***Ballad Of The Landlord*** (p.54) Langston Hughes is one of America's best-known poets. His main subject for over forty years until his death in 1967 was the experience of black people living in the USA.

Mama Dot (p.26) Ashante is a region in central Ghana that was suppressed by the British in 1900. Fred D'Aguiar was born in London of Guyanese parents, but he grew up in Guyana then returned to London in 1972. Through the character of 'Mama Dot' he writes about the experiences of black people living in Britain.

Reception (p.28) Colin Bartlett contributed this poem to the BBC Writers' Weekly programme, in a series for new poets. Prison blues are prison uniform.

In My Country (p.29) John Vorster was a South African statesman who supported and enforced apartheid.

The Censor (p.30) Ivan Kraus (1939–) was born in Prague, which he left after the Russian invasion of 1968, to live in France and Germany. 'The Censor' was first performed in a dance programme, before being published as a poem. A censor is an official who examines books and films and decides whether parts are not suitable for the public to see and should be taken out.

The Burning Of The Books (p.31) Book-burning has been carried out by many systems of government throughout history, including the Nazi Party. It is a way of getting rid of any books that are seen to criticize the government. It is also a way of showing the power of that government to the people.

The Need For Censorship (p.32) Reiner Kunze (1933–) was born in Delsmitz, Germany. His work was banned in East Germany when he protested against the Russian invasion of Czechoslovakia. Eventually he was expelled from the East German Writers' Union and moved to Greiz in West Germany, where he now lives.

Search (p.33) Yannis Ritsos was imprisoned in 1948, during the period of the second Civil War in Greece, then again in 1967, when the country was governed by a small 'junta' of army colonels. His works were banned during the whole of the period from 1936 to 1952, then again under the colonels. It didn't prevent his poetry from being widely known, especially that set to music by Theodorakis.

Hope (p.34), **His Eye Is On The Sparrow** (p.36) A military group under General Pinochet seized power in Chile in 1973. During the next few years they were responsible for the arrest and imprisonment of thousands of people. Many disappeared and were never heard of again. Relatives of many of the 'disappeared' are still searching for clues about what happened to them. The Villa Grimaldi, the Colonia Dignidad and Londres Street were notorious detention centres where many people were tortured. The Junta was a law-making council.

Twenty Comrades (p.38), **I Shall Sing** (p.39) The Palestinian writer Fouzi El-Asmar was arrested in 1969 by the Israelis and imprisoned for 15 months. In 1972 he went to live in the United States.

Pawiak 1943 (p.40) Pawiak was the Nazi prison in Warsaw, Poland, during the Second World War. It is now a war memorial and museum. Jerzy Ficowski (1924–) served in the Polish army in the Second World War and much of his poetry was about the suffering of the victims of war.

La Libertad (p.41) The name of a prison in Uruguay.

The Most Unbelievable Part (p.42) Marjorie Agosin (1954–) is a Chilean poet who now lives in the United States.

Strong Men Destroy A City (p.44) Solon (630–c.560 BC) was an ancient Greek statesman and poet. As a statesman, he introduced more humane laws and worked hard to get rid of poverty.

Somoza Unveils the Statue of Somoza in Somoza Stadium (p.45) General Somoza seized power in Nicaragua in 1935, and was president until 1956. His son was president for most of the time until 1979, when revolution and civil war broke out. A new government, the Sandinistas, took over in 1980. Ernesto Cardenal (1925–) is a revolutionary poet and Roman Catholic priest. He played an active part in the revolution that brought down Somoza in 1979.

Sonnet: England in 1819 (p.46) Percy Shelley (1792–1822) was a romantic poet. He strongly believed in freedom for all people, no matter what their status was. The poem refers to King George III of Britain, who by this time was mad and unable to govern the country properly. Liberticide means the destruction of freedom.

The Stalin Epigram (p.47) Osip Mandelstam was arrested after the Russian authorities heard about this poem about Stalin, the leader of the Soviet Union. The poem itself was not written down, but a few people memorized it. It is possible that an agent of the KGB (the Russian secret police) heard it recited. Mandelstam died in a camp in Siberia, a vast, desolate region, probably in 1937.

The Hand That Signed The Paper (p.48) Dylan Thomas (1914–53) was a Welsh poet and writer. His best-known work is

his play for voices *Under Milk Wood*.

Description Of An Idea (p.49) Bruce Dawe (1930–) is thought of as Australia's most popular poet. He was born in Geelong, and worked at a variety of jobs before taking up teaching and writing.

Refugee Blues (p.50) W H Auden (1907–73) was one of the best-known English poets of his time. He lived for many years in America, becoming a US citizen in 1946.

The Little Cart (p.52) Chēn Tzŭ-lung was born in 1607. He became a high-ranking soldier, and helped the Ming princes against the advancing Manchus. He was caught by Manchu soldiers, and drowned while trying to escape.

From: To The Dead Poor Man (p.56) Pablo Neruda (1904–73) was a poet, diplomat and Marxist. He won the Nobel Prize for Literature in 1971 and the Lenin Prize for Peace in 1953. He was fiercely critical of the oppressive right-wing regime in Chile after 1948, when he was forced into hiding.

Here Is Klito's Little Shack (p.57) Leonidas, who lived in the third century BC, was a Greek epigrammatist, writing verses in memory of people who had died.

A Village (p.58) Ana Blandiana (1942–) is a Romanian writer. She began to write her poetry in the years after the release of thousands of political prisoners in 1964. She is one of the most widely read Romanian poets.

Peace (p.59) Ritsos wrote this after his release from prison in 1953.

INDEX OF FIRST LINES